Through all the Displacements

poems by
Edgar Gabriel Silex

CURBSTONE PRESS

Printed in the U.S. on acid-free paper by BookCrafters
Cover art: Robert W. Two Bulls
Cover design: Stephanie Church

Curbstone Press is a 501(c)(3) nonprofit publishing house
whose operations are supported in part by private donations
and by grants from ADCO Foundation, J. Walton Bissell
Foundation, Inc., Witter Bynner Foundation for Poetry, Inc.,
Connecticut Commission on the Arts, Connecticut Arts
Endowment Fund, The Ford Foundation, The Greater
Hartford Arts Council, Lannan Foundation, LEF Foundation,
Lila Wallace-Reader's Digest Literary Publishers Marketing
Development Program, administered by the Council of
Literary Magazines and Presses, The Andrew W. Mellon
Foundation, National Endowment for the Arts-Literature,
National Endowment for the Arts International Projects
Initiative and The Plumsock Fund.

Library of Congress Cataloging-in-Publication Data

Silex, Edgar
    Through all the displacements / by Edgar Gabriel Silex.
      p.   cm.
    ISBN 1-880684-25-X
    1. Indians of North America—Poetry. 2. Yana Indians—Poetry.
    I. Title.
    PS3569.I4216T48 1995
    811'.54—dc20   95-30112

published by
CURBSTONE PRESS   321 Jackson Street   Willimantic, CT 06226

To everything that is Past and Now
— Bert, Danny, Ishi —
which is woven in Tomorrow,
in my son, Gabriel.

ACKNOWLEDGMENTS

Thanks to the National Endowment for the Arts and the
Maryland State Arts Council for their support.

Thanks to Heather Davis for her invaluable editing, to Michael
Collier for his faith, and to Lauren for everything.

Additional thanks to the following publications in which some of
these poems first appeared, sometimes in earlier versions:
*The Americas Review, Birmingham Poetry Review, Chants, Chiron
Review, Coffeehouse Poet's Quarterly, Dancing Shadow Review,
Detonation of the Voice, GYST, The Haight Ashbury Literary
Journal, The Hispanic Culture Review, Hitchhiker Magazine, New
Sins Press, Red Dirt, Slipstream, Una Mas Magazine, Left Curve,
Poetry Like Bread Anthology, Maryland Poetry Review*

PREFACE

Some of these poems refer to Ishi, the last Native American who lived as Native Americans lived before the arrival of Europeans. Ishi was a member of the Yahi, a tribe of the Yana Nation. After gold was discovered in California and the gold rush began, the entire Yana Nation of 3,000 people was systematically exterminated in the span of one year. Ishi, and about a dozen Yahi, managed to hide and survive for about forty years on what remained of their mountainous land. After everyone had died he continued to live in solitude for three years. He was found, nearly starved to death, on a farm in Oroville, California in 1911, where he had wandered from what appeared to be sheer loneliness. Ishi was placed in a jail cell for two weeks because they did not know what to do with him. A professor of anthropology took him under his care. He was placed in a museum of anthropology as a living *artifact*. He lived there for four and half years until his death from tuberculosis.

One poem refers to La Llorona, a southwestern myth of a woman who drowned her children and is condemned to walk the earth. Eternally crying out their names, she searches the rivers for their bodies. The myth derives from the conquest when most Native Americans were enslaved by the Spanish. They used mercury to extract the gold and silver from mines where they worked as forced labor. In 1619, Juan de Solorzano wrote, "the [mercury] poison penetrated to the very marrow, debilitating all members and causing a constant shaking, and the workers usually died within four years." In *The Indians of the Americas*, John Collier writes, "as Indian manpower died off, Indian women were put into the mines more ruthlessly, working in knee-deep water through the coldest season of the year...those yet living were forced to pay tribute for the dead...mothers killed their children rather than let them be taken to the mines." In this tragedy lies the root of La Llorona.

CONTENTS

Shadows of Words

Remembering Ishi (? - March 25, 1916)

through grainy images
and intermittent visions
through thousand-year-old stories
retold to me as a child
as if they happened yesterday
through my grandfather's elucidations
through my distrust

of the shadows of words
through my reservations
my relations   and gaps
through all the displacements
and the exact orders of histories
through the miscellaneous occurrences
and the presumptions

that multiplied   subdued
and now have dominion
over what was once free
through violence I've suffered
and its erasure by victory
through the refractions of Time
through all the reasons I've heard

and their inconsistencies
the horror of remembering is all I seek
in order to remember well   Ishi
in order that I might gain some
indifference

The Unwelcomed Tune of God

Cuidad Juarez: July 1992

after 34 years of listening
I realize He does not always sing
welcoming songs of morning birds
or Gregorian chants of solemn death
sometimes He hums an onerous tune

metered and measured in sufferance
and who can say that is not His song too
who can say that was not His voice
crying at the corner of Diez y Seis
de Septiembre and Francisco Villa

near the open mercado cradled in the arms
of one who could be my indigent mother
who wore black Indian braids
and squatted on her sidewalk home
who can say that was not His unwelcome tune

the melody of a two-day-old's cries
as he vomited milk mixed with blood
I heard His lyrics in a concerned
shopkeeper's voice asking
que le pasa a su niño   ésta enfermo

I heard His sad beat beating
my thoughts into prayers as I strolled
by toward the tourist mercado
pretending to be unconscious   I heard
His rhythm in my footsteps sustained

by the long awful acceptance
that I must not stop
that I must not stop
that I must keep His rhythm
especially in this haunted immanent city

11

Cuauhtemoc—The Last Emperor

Cuauhtemoc was the last Aztec Emperor

he lies on his right side on the store stoop
uses the 'A' section of *El Fronterizo*
for sheets and covers

he feels the missing-tooth gap with his tongue
his matted straight black hair is too long
for this heat   he perspires

today was definitely not his birthday
with the Spanish kids who stole
his twelve begged pesos

and the mestizo who chased and kicked him
for stealing a churro from the kiosk
but when he saw him fly like that

not much force behind the kick
he got that look of remorse
and let him have the churro anyway

then he gave that same remorseful look
to Amaranto's pleading eyes
and was forced to offer his last two bites

his rib cage is blue and red around the edges
more swollen than earlier   it aches to breath
he must try not to roll in his sleep

rubbing the shiny tooth in his right hand
that fell out when he landed
he wonders what being lost means

if it is the same as the feeling he got
when his little brother failed to wake up
last winter   he wonders when his birthday is

feeling the ivory smooth baby tooth
between his thumb and finger
maybe tomorrow is his birthday

he tries to imagine what it might bring
rain perhaps   a cool day   a dozen tortillas
he closes his brown eyes

listens to the other Indians huddled
up the street of La Reforma Bulevar
he doesn't remember why he understands

Indians   their language a mix of Indian words
with Spanish   a baby cries far off
as he falls into the dreams of children

The Planting of the Blue Corn

after the fields are planted
and the blue corn seeds are nestled
in the red earth   after the Corn Planter
has put away his sacred planting stick
he says a prayer to the quiet air
that hovers above the lines
marking the seeded fields

and then the wind puts on
its dancing moccasins and begins
to swirl   to spin above
the cleared and pregnant naked land
brushing up the red dust
from its grounded desert feet

and together they begin a choreographed
whirling and swinging
like little tornados pirouetting
together they marionette above
the corn rows   and the clouds

wishing not to be left out
begin to clap in rhythm
to the thrum of the rustling
sage leaves   and everyone
starts dancing in the dust of happiness

the mountains and the trees rattle
with the increasing crescendo
of the clapping clouds and the tumbleweeds
start rolling in a joyous laughter
and the clouds   too   begin to laugh
until their joyous tears fall
sending everyone scurrying away

from the planting festival below
and the dust lies back down
and the wind blows away
in search of other pregnant fields
and the rain falls
and the blue corn shoots
begin to grow

Postcard

just a quick note Ishi

I took my son to the Museum of Natural History
we looked disquietly for your long black hair
in the glass encasements of mothballed worlds
we listened for the clacking speech of your bones
among the fossils of grandfather-whales
who still sing their ancient songs
into the awestruck eyes of children

we did not find you amid the white
tanned-painted mannequins dressed
like powwow tourists in sacred clothes
nor were you one of the Melanesians
Africans or Aboriginals standing stiffly
and dusty like taxidermic trophies

there were no Vikings or Druids
making human sacrifices   pillaging
the corners of a yet undying world
which left us chary of all the exclusions
still   we did not find you weaving
baskets or chipping arrowheads stored among silk
plants and crowds too noisy to hear
the wind caressing the mountains
of your Yana tomb   so we left saddened

because even here   among the trophy cases
the strand of web that wove your people
was cut from the fabric of this torn world
secretly   we were glad not to find you
frozen there   still weaving and carving
looking like Spider Woman cocooned
in her own web

Blue Cloud Rides Horses

blue cloud rides horses behind the wheel
of his chevy el camino with the hurst
four-on-the-floor

blue cloud rides psychedelic horses
and some made of remembered pain

blue cloud rides horses that leave hoof trails
up and down his atrophic veins

blue cloud rides cell block horses
made of steel bars and thick walls
and when he gets out he rides horses again

blue cloud rides his baby's horse
and it makes him cry and it makes him cry
and it makes him want to forget
and makes him want and want and nearly die of want

blue cloud rides horses he thinks he hates
named officer   custer   john smith
de soto   jefferson   jackson   lincoln
columbus   cortez   and BIA

blue cloud rides horses he remembers he loved
named gin for the father he loved
named wild irish rose for the mother he loved

blue cloud rides ephemeral horses
sewn from dreamskin and old chants
named blue cloud and red cloud and white cloud
and grey clouds that rain faded dreams

blue cloud rides wind war-horses
on the ghost breezes
of the little big horn's plains
and he always wins   and he always wins

blue cloud rides horses that ride him
harder and faster to the vanishing haze

Laughter

I laugh at everything
everything has a funny bone
I laugh when I'm asked
what is your Indian name
as if every Indian has one

or when I was asked for a tie—
as if a tie can be a passport
to a forbidden world—
I would go get a tie   then a coat
then they would say   there's no more room
I went home laughing and laughing

I remember laughing when the white cops beat us
we were handcuffed to a barbed wire fence
thought we stole some car stereo
my cousin said   my grandma hits harder than that
we laughed and laughed

as their fists bruised our bodies
as they tried harder   not to kill us
they took our money   dumped us in the desert
we laughed like coyotes at the craziest moon

I laugh at everything
because unintentionally I bang into things
like when I bang my funny bone
and it goes numb from the pain

my cousin   he's doing ten-to-twenty
for riding the horse through his veins too long
and for giving the cops such a good time

I'm unemployed   doing life in the mortgage
recalling the world I wanted to change
so I still have lots of reason to laugh

sometimes he calls me from Huntsville
and we laugh together
at the failures we've made of ourselves

The Note Left on a Reservation

for Charles Simic

I saw God dressed in long black braids return
500 years worth of his salary to a man who lost
the money in a church where he slunk in to hide
it like an unrepented sin in the heel of his black boot

I saw a huge tarantula slowly cross an intersection
it could have been at the Tigua reservation
or at the center of a sacred web

I saw a spirit form from 99.9 percent of every creation
the rest was composed from my faith manifesting
just long enough to convince me of my vision

I heard a poor poet recite nearly all the laws of God
with one spoken glance of his humble eyes

The Horse Trade

I

Abel wears black   plays Bogus Charlie
games with the horse traders
squatting on the tumbleweed lawn
of an adobe shack built by the Spanish
slavers before Popéy drove them from our land
during the Pueblo revolt

I've got two stolen Broncos
still unbroken as the odometer reads
Able translates the trading conditions
for these two American workhorses
with the tinted eyes and the pop-off heads
he tells them they are worth at least
two ounces of sweet brown flesh-
eating horse

the morning sun slants our eyes
which we use to listen cautiously
to the unuttered speech that bodies speak
or to the wind who might carry our talk
out to the parks where the needlejockies itch
fidgeting a hair trigger urge for a fix
or where *chotas* circle like great whites
handing out 30 year passes to the brick

II

Ishi   you were only the first of the last
tribes who cling to this desert of microchip factories
asphalt snakes and electronic surveillance machines

nothing has changed Ishi
the burning for gold has stopped   now
they rape for uranium   fight electronic wars for oil

swindle for any undervalued company
that can transform angels into seraphims
and I don't know what this lingering
in the fire-water world means anymore

III

we Pueblos are corn-sowing people
but we have always been good traders
we traded horses with Cochise
Geronimo   Ten Bears   with Mangas Coloradas
before they branded his feet
put four bullets in his severed head
and sold his scalp to the Mexicans
for one hundred dollars

today we trade two Broncos
with some faceless Federales
who confiscated a pound of horse
from some gringos at the border
we will sell it for profit   to people
suffering to exit this world
which Able and I have learned to embrace

Police (*Chota*)

Another 'Because' Poem

because the baby would not stop crying
and their methadone had just kicked in
and they couldn't wait to lick
each other's prison tattoos
she and her lover quieted the baby forever
with a sip of methadone

because the Navaho did not have enough money to pay
and the white cashier chose to return the Wild Turkey
in defiance he left the milk and eggs
and took the hot dogs the bread and the Wild Turkey
with the two Dreamsicles and the two Milky Ways
that brought large smiles to his kids

because a Mexican who did not know
if he was Mixteca or Azteca
stopped me in a boondock town in Nebraska
on a cold winter day without a coat
and asked if I spoke spanish
if I knew where he could work for food
or if I knew where those train tracks went

because history disappears too quickly
and if what happened to Mangas Coloradas
to Moctezuma   Geronimo in the circus
in The Long Walk   the price of an Indian scalp
to Kintpuash or to Spotted Elk
lying frozen in the snow beside his wife and children
in the blessed ground of Wounded Knee
if those things disappear too quickly
then who will remember what a swastika means

because 500 years have passed
and the end is still ending
in the Guatemalan and Peruvian countrysides
riddled with Indian corpses

because culture is not something we pass on
but something we chose to live within
the day will come when my son will have to choose
to love or hate the color of his father's skin
because Ishi was not the last of the last
as he was never first of the last

because our erasers are needles
and glue and spray paint
or else our memories of defiance

because I have two sisters
being erased by the words and fists of men

because I had two brothers
who erased themselves

because last night when the stars seem so beautiful
I still dreamed of my death

View From a Red Topped Mountain

beyond a red topped mountain   a chasm and a second mountain
the desert stretches   thermals shimmer like windswept oceans
below   to the curve and each sacred corner   stunted mesquite
are spilled jade buttons or men kneeling forever kissing the ground

my sister tells us she bought back these few acres of red sand
on blistering days you can see our grandfathers searching for roots
setting jackrabbit traps   painting our faces on faces of cliffs
here are the hawks and vultures   here is a human's home

along the horizon   green lush   roofs   pools   asphalt snakes
slither down mountains into the sprawl surrounding Fort Bliss
along mountain ridges dust devils rise and duck spot and trace
something like ghost warriors measuring the cavalry

Extinctions

grandmother forgets my son's name
her eyes search inward   then looks beyond me
expects a Delphic wind to whisper
his name   I am the wind
recalling it for her

he drank the night into oblivion
pissed its memory into the toilet
often   when he wakes   he wants to reach
into the city's bowels   reclaim the nights
he can't remember

Nieves speaks perfect Spanish
likes to blow air-kisses
she dyes her hair blond
to lighten the darkness
of her Indian skin

he buries his tongue beneath English syntax
and the serial cognition of Greek syllogisms
but when he hears a single immutable word
from his forsaken language
his bones rattle as if they understand

beneath the Spanish cathedrals
of Mexico City   Tenochtitlan sinks
back into the navel of its Indian birth

when he had his mistress over
he hid every evidence of his wife
until his wife no longer existed
even after he put everything back

he stopped me in a crowded subway
two Indians in a darkened tunnel
what Nation are you from he asked
America I said   Peru he said
we disappeared into the crowd
searching for separate exits

every day a child memorizes an old Greek myth
as he forgets a step of a native custom
every day one culture shoves another
the mutable moves toward the edges   beyond memory
so that eventually everyone is uncertain
if they are assimilating or reversing Babel

Eternity

soft curves of sand
bodies lying in the sun   mirage
of thorn people   settling wandering
becoming their own eluvial earth

on moonless skies owls witch
and ghosts roam the echolessness
awakened by the windy sounds of oceans
or perhaps the human cries of coyote puppies

here the crown-of-thorns has always bloomed
its leaves turning to red tear blossoms
here in sagebrush shadows serpents dream
of the rain's voice   of Eden   of seduction

and from the blue sea above the world is scrutinized
through the clear-eyed windows of winged feifdoms
listen   from beyond the melting horizon it comes
the mock laughter of twin thunder gods

Washington, D.C.

it is not a place
where the dead can be buried
they would not rest like stones
it is not a place where the air sings
the Potomac licks blood off its banks
I have walked its red rivers
16th Street NW   Pennsylvania Avenue SE
I have seen the white stone faces staring
from marble sepulchres memorializing the sacred
names of slavers and lynchmen

I have heard moccasin bells
ringing the night   echodancing
against red brick walls and white columns
those dance steps were not my own
but those of Red Cloud
of Red Bird of Hollow Horn Bear
of Standing Bear   of Ten Bears
of Santanta of Muskogees
of Sauk of Cheyenne of Mandans
Choctaws   Blackfeet   Anacostans
Bear Clans Fox Clans *Ishi*
of clans whose names only the wind sings now

by day   I can see crow people
perched in the windows of the Treasury
the Capitol   the Archives   I walk fast
this place is not for the living
when I walk over manhole covers
I can still hear deceptions
conspiring whispers that steal
through catacombs   seeping up through street cracks
until they mix with the holy bloodstream
of women   children   and warriors
and the blood of others I am not familiar with

in the night
before the shadows of crows can be seen
in front of the Supreme Court
I have heard ephemeral pleadings
rattling the sarcophagus' doors
even the fish have swum downstream
to saltier waters that don't taste of blood
when I walk the red rivers
I am reminded of the dead who live here
about danger of ghosts
who breathe the black air
who walk in my nightmares
I know   even the dead have memories
I know   that is what keeps spirits here
this is their city now
this is their City of Death

Man (*Ishi*— Yana word)

Leaving Cibola

El Paso, Texas is the last place Francisco Vasquez
de Coronado searched for the Seven Cities of
Cibola. He established two missions to convert the
Indians. The missions are still active as are the
unconverted tribes.

no one has ever left here not even Coronado
who came with delusions of cibolas
to claim a desert of gold
who can be found ragged and unshaven
waiting with other drunken Tiguas
in the soup line of the Ysleta mission

and the missionaries who came with him
to nail Indians to crosses
their ghostly voices can also be heard
near the river at night baptizing
young Indian women with their sperm

sometimes in the desert sunlight
the red sand-ghost warriors will dance
in a swirl of dust devil happiness
as if time was unchanged
as if the Pueblo revolt had just ended

in the hot summer if you look into the distant
mirages you may see
the conquistadores in their shiny armor
riding their horses toward the glint
of downtown glass monuments
they never found a single grain
of sacred dust gold or otherwise

as I drive out of the mountainous arms
hugging this dust bowl   I see red
canyon fingers   soft palms of earth
cradling the lives of a hunched-over people
deluded by the illusions of glass mirrored cities
of American riches they cannot find
having already lost and forgotten
how to be Tiguas Aztecas Mixcos Poconchis Yaqui-Tepeus

in the rearview mirror I watch cibola
fading at night   glimmering like the sweat of my people
and I know where the gold is   and where it will remain

Metis Medicine Blanket

you could say we were unsure of ourselves
it was a lighter skin
             an unfamiliar god
that we sought
        as if in someone else's idea
in someone else's cabin
          in the frozen reaches
            we would find
what we lost in our trail of sorrow
            what was erased by the cross
of flesh
        that crushed an old world
but whose scraps were used to build anew

and we wrapped our flesh with this
            infested blanket given to us
because it was the only way
          to find warmth
and survive long enough
          to unravel
    the mysteries that enveloped us
and soon   we realized
         the blanket was sewn from notions
stranded like strings of sand
        that rubbed our bodies
and sanded our eyes
  until it smoothed out all of our doubts
and we were as polished as our axioms
Thunder Mountain-Shiprock-The Black Hills
        Tenochtitlan
and we discovered ourselves again
     rising out of lakes and rivers
out of earth navels
         feathered in quetzal
stalking like jaguars

through jungles of coyote nights
calling ourselves
        not someone else's
invalidations of us
    not Chicano   Hispanic   Latino
but Nations of Repossessed Histories
    who dance and speak in tongues
as if Columbus had never been here
  as if this repossession had never been
this New World's   most frightening dream

To Benedictus De Spinoza

Benedictus   if I could only believe
in your spiritual freedom   long ago I accepted
the unchanging order of this stoic world
not just as a form of ultimate beauty
but as the reason behind my own prosaic existence

finding hope in the institutions
of industry   marriage and family
I shunned the secular and the religious
orders of myths   you could say I clung to the primitive
skills innate to any parent   like Aristotle
I held to the substance and its empirical truths

always uneasy with the ineffable
I began to accept fate as the natural order
an acceptance which you believed in a fate-ruled world
would be man's only means to spiritual freedom
I was even undaunted by the mystery of coincidence
which I assumed to be a test of my faith

I dreamed of nothing unattainable
forged a world in my mind incorruptible
by the absence of God   in a disposable world
one disposes of all reasons for God
I said without shame   God was nothing
and if God was nothing   I was nothing
that meant everything to me

but freedom is an illusive spirit   Benedictus
mine is caught in a Dœdalus web of everyday errands
of parental instincts   and I am ashamed
of how it grips me   of how I never lowered my eyes
to a grander humility   uncomfortable in the umbrous
embrace of abstractions and notions
I am afraid to admit to myself that I am a figment

looming over the mystery who wears my face
who travels city to city   bedroom to bedroom   lost
in the carnal   in the insignificant   in the daily
pragmatisms of survival   my spirit has become red brick
and white marble columns mirroring my world   and God
is a greener notion   less immune to ineffability

you say a mind is but one word   one thought
one piece of an infinite substance
you called the mind of God   if it is so
then I feel as if I am but one doubt in God's mind
as if I am His fate questioning His own existence
implying His infinite possibility for imperfection

like the first human who wishing to be a human being
searched the forest for a spirit
but the sound of footsteps sent the spirits scurrying
to the treetops   afraid but undaunted by his attraction
to their eternal songs   he reached one
only to discover his touch turned them into birds
and they flew off as prayers of his soul

that is all I am left with   Benedictus
the image that I am a human living in a forest
bounded by my fear of the power of words
by my attraction to the shadow of each word
when I reach and touch one I know
that as in the beginning God is the word
connecting me to my own imperfection
and impermanence

Remembering

"I can report the case of an old prospector-pioneer-miner-trapper of this region [Butte County], who had on his bed even in recent years a blanket lined with Indian scalps. These had been taken years before. He had never been a government scout, soldier, or officer of the law. The Indians he had killed purely on his own account. No reckoning was at any time demanded of him."
—Theodora Kroeber
excerpt from, *Ishi: Between Two Worlds*

some remember through daguerreotypes
of Edward Curtis and Walter McClintock
some are consumed by visions
retelling thousand-year-old stories
as if they were recent accounts
some listen to their grandfather's
elucidations
as others find their memories by distrusting
the shadows of words

some reconstruct mosaic memories
by their reservations   relations and gaps
rediscovering themselves in the displacements
in the exact orders of histories
in the miscellaneous shards scattered throughout

some have learned to remember by not remembering
the presumptions that have multiplied   subdued
and now have dominion over their memories

even through violence and its erasure by victory
even through the refractions of Time
through all the inconsistent reasoning
the horror of remembering is all they seek
in order that they might gain
some indifference

The Bodies of Shadows

Grandfather Buffalo

I saw them staring at him
in the mall   I was small
holding his granite hand
his skin was bronzed
straight blue-black hair
his eyes and nose slightly curved
towards earth

I knew what was in their stares
an old Indian coin
a fat-lipped feathered caricature
a Cleveland team name
a wooden carving in an antique store
the relief of a bygone bus token
they saw the logo of Omaha
sponsor of nature shows
visions of Geronimo
parading in the circus
they were unbelieving
first-time gazes
colored by amazement

truth looked like a buffalo
a tall wide block that walks
like a stampede   desert soil skin
lungs that puff great mists
and appaloosa legs
that can outrun tornadoes

grandfather Buffalo
never stared back
never turned back the stares
of the wake we made
in our stampeding walk
through the mall

La Llorona's House — 1959

the moon's crescent fingers slip
into the black nightwaters
bringing with them memories
of drowning in madness
where I sank tonight
and saw her in that fiery world
with her severed head clenched

in her hand by the locks of her red hair
where I heard her sad mouth
still crying for us as she walked
the esplanade where she drowned
our childhoods   where she drowned
you in the broom closet
behind the heavy bureau holding the door

muffling your cry-gasps your sighs
for redemption   songs of a three-year-old
boy cast from his heaven   confused
by his mother's confusions
you were in there three days
and two nights held down
with the hungry lions   we smelled

your discomfort   heard your tears
never sleeping   knew God had come
to console you   heard Him whispering
in the playful voice of a child
murmuring your little boy games
down in the edgeless darkness
of the drowning room

For Bert

The Untied

the wife

her tongue douses
for every quiver   every moan   every hip gyration
she wastes no time in finding me
and her act of love is done

her life traces
every breath where she longs
to find me finding her where I have never found her
finding out her self

the mistresses

this one is the lonely eyes of my childhood
every kiss I give kisses the orphan in my past
turns the nights into enveloping mothers
until daylight shines upon my lie

this one is the flesh that loves fleshings
has no preference for its forms or obligations
as long as I blush and laugh and moan
from pleasure and not from some remembered pain

this one knows only that she fell in love
by flesh or by words   by my truths and my lies
but that doesn't matter any more
all that matters is her wait

the husband

I cannot remember if she has one face or many
if she was me or I was her   sometimes I don't know
where the ends are to all my lives
or how I've watched them moan

arch their backs lift their thighs against my chest
waited for them to burst in silent flames
waited for my turn   to imagine my wife
and how it leaves me empty in the end

1964

remember the day
I was in second grade you were in fourth
and the world's misery was still covered
in iridescence before I got pneumonia
and heard the sweet drowning voice of death

that was the day you said let's play hooky
I said —Okay! thinking of horse games we played
on our way to school   we ate our lunch
for breakfast spent our 50 cents of milk money
at señora Torre's candy store
she was making big fat red delicious candy apples
like shiny red crystal balls we could have looked into
and seen our reddish future

we sat on the levee
beneath a sunlight we had never imagined before
eating our Payday bars   our Bar-B-Q Lays potato chips
drinking our Pepsi's last as we watched
our bronze people lift their dreams up
to keep the river from drowning them
carrying them with all their skills on their backs

we never got to eat our candy apples
because the Border Patrol came thought we were Mexicans
when the truant officer took us home grandma covered us
with red welts from grandpa's belt
before we were put in separate rooms to cry
like we would always cry   by ourselves

that was the best day of our schooling
we learned school was meant to keep us
from seeing that sunlight created this world
school would shape our eyes
into prisms that could split the brilliance

so that everything we saw we would see through
pigments and shadows and the memory of light
would be lost from our eyes   that day
when we touched the ache of this world
we learned the secret of why some people fulfill
their own wishes to die

For Bert

Coyotes

after the fifty-cent wrestling matches
at the county coliseum
grandpa and I walked home
like coyotes in the desert dusk
prowling beneath sapphire skies

holding his warm chiseled hand
I remember running my nails
across the ribs of his calloused palm
and thinking of the frontdoor screen

we seldom broke the quiet
with our voices
stars like shimmering snowflakes
slowly descended in the night's horizon
holding us in wild contentment

making us feel like howling
into the balmy air
making us feel like running
with our noses just above the sand
around tumbleweeds and sage
sniffing for sounds of life
flushing out others frozen
by the flickering sapphires in the sky

it was a long silent way to our house
only our footsteps could be heard
crunching quartz and coral sand grains
the silence never bothered us
no anxiety   just warm hands held
walking   sniffing   a still night
and coyotes beneath sapphire skies

1973

I think of your uncareful life
racing 383 cubic inches
of four-barrel-fuel-injected
steel muscle combustion
straight toward parked cars
at eighty miles an hour
and not veering
until you were sure
we had seen our death

and I think of your defying dives
from 50 foot tree branches
into the narrowest creek
that dared us
beyond our recklessness

when you did not come up
we would dive in
but only to save ourselves
from you
over and over again
until we tired
of saving

you danced like a moon
waxing   then   waning
across your own dark sky
pulled on the tight strings
of the broken the abused
of gravity

o how we desired you
as if by being near you
we could near our impossibilities

we all wanted uncareful lives
so we could be as free as you
but with each phase
of your full and bright exhilaration
or your dark and abject loneliness
we could see you
were the sacrificial lamb
of our vicarious lives

For Bert

Inaccurate Love Notes

You give your heart to one thing after another.
Carrying, you do not carry it.
— Nahua poem

You haven't called in a week   she says
as I run my finger along her bust   she adds
excursively   I'm glad I have breasts
they make you so happy

I have lost the means to defend myself
against my self-denials   on my way home
I put the cartop down   think of the time I need
to work on these neglections   at the stoplight

in the car beside me   I see them staring at me
perhaps the one next to me sees through me
she licks her lips slowly   the driver says something
they all smile and laugh

the one in back rolls down the window   says
in a voice just loud enough for me   I want
to be fucked by you   I keep my eyes ahead   grin
when the light turns I gun ahead of them

at home I sit in silence remembering how
last night it happened again   her face was eyeless
mouthless   noseless   once   I got tired
of making up lies but when I spoke the truth
it did not feel like it   souls are like that
they want to feel their truthfulness yet be free of it

one year I put on weight to avoid the seduction
of glances   now I just admit I have other women
set myself up to envy the way they still accept me
or to covet the ache I get when they're indifferent

I believe in not hurting anyone   I tell one
though when they call I can't say no
you remind me of a woman she says   things happen
to you like they happen to women except   perhaps
not as scary — but it's not them who scare me

I tie someone to the bed put a scarf around her eyes
when she whispers   what are you going to do to me
my flesh knows what my thoughts can't answer
quiet I say you mustn't talk
she tastes and smells the same   but inside
each corner each fold every large and small
contraction is as different as the others

I remember hearing her gleaming in her high heels
upstairs in our house trying on this and that
I   patiently waiting beside her box
filled with molded rubber
this one has a sleekness I envy
that one she got for its curve
this one and that one frighten me
I hear her cautiously descending
entering the room smiling and drink-happy
how she liked to dress up for all her toys

you're shy she says that's how you make friends
by having sex with them late at night
in the circle of her arms she asks me what love means
I say I think love is learning
to forgive though not always knowing why

then I remember how once I survived on the gratitude
of a marriage that fell to those indescribable desires
which keep changing every time I think I've found someone
who might define them

The Drowning

what warning did you get from me
night crawler
beware of stealthy sea slugs
how you must have hooked him
with your meathook breasts
with your coral jewel
long before the horns had sounded
how could we pursue our dreams
with all the waves rolling from your bedroom
with all the memories of drowning

did you not hear us suffocating in your tides
lapping at the walls of our rooms
you creaking that square island with him
as we slipped down fathoms of innocence
we thought he was the only sea slug
who went from his abysm to your room
until we heard your doorknob snick
and you worming towards his
that snick shucked Daniel into suicide and I
I waited to be dissolved to sand

while each night you slithered out
of your ocean with evasive eyes and the fear
of mutant sea slugs growing
inside you   your hisses pleading
me to speak for you   to sink down   down
to his abysmal room   to say   to drown
to say   to drown   in what was till then unspoken
oceans between your brother and your father

   For Danny Boy

Fathers

there is a time to be silent   he said
on our longest drive home   enveloped
in spoken glances   in a closeness
where I lost a childhood   and we became more men
than we would ever be   my father and I

it is the way of men   to speak in pauses
between what we say   controlling how we say
the few words we choose   between fathers and sons
between an old man   and a brand new man
between old wounds   and our fear of the next

I stood close to him   as morning slowly fell
squatting our shadows   blending us
while he watered the lawn   he never seeded or watered
he even cooked breakfast

things I unvaryingly did   for him
for my brother and sister   because
he was always someplace else   because
in his absence   I had become the father
I always dreamed for   the father

now waiting   in that silence of men
for a slight wind   to explain
the fear he seeded   inside my sister
a short wind   carrying the silence
we would take to our deaths

The Truth

perhaps you can find the truth studying Einstein
or how Socrates deduced it out of the Delphic demiurge
I remember the truths I was coerced to memorize
there are five oceans   five continents   I remember them
like a swallow remembers the spring   even with eyes closed

I can still see the proof in the blue circular perfection
its five distinct Turtle Islands   and I was amazed
at how truths could be so mistrusting after Europe
became a sixth continent between my third and fourth grades
I know truths do not hold well to empirical scrutiny

nondescript   noumenal   they soar beyond man's logic
but they can be tested   like my grandfather compelled me to
over years   when he whispered seeds in my mind—
organized religion enslaves this world   he said
turning all my philosophies into origins of disbelief

where a new search begins   which has been joyfully bitter
though what's most painful is knowing that by knowing the truth
I lose more than my ignorance   a part of my innocence too
but that's what convinced Einstein to become a pacifist
and gave Socrates dignity as he drank that potion of death

January 1977

he was on military leave on his way
to the funeral of our little brother's suicide

he pulled over in Oklahoma
under a big old tree

firstborns understand
something about suicidal brothers

perhaps the lonely ache of blue flesh
or the crushing of a father's ridicule

perhaps it's the endless days
full of such self-lacerations

I heard someone cut him down
gave him back his breath

but the black and blue noose slowly tightened
for three long years

until he must have known his suicide
would save me from mine

    For Danny Boy and Bert

The Birthday — August 25, 1980

all my life I wanted a brother
not the one I had
not the one who lived
in a separate world like I did

I wanted the brother who defended me
against Freddy the *Chango* and Jaíme Portillo
against Califas and all those white guys
who called me spic and mule-headed injun

I wanted the brother who loved Roberto Duran
who would come to my lonely apartment
to watch his fights on TV
I wanted the brother I spoke with by glance
by the tones of words that brothers speak

I didn't want the brother of our father's fists
because I cried when he couldn't
in my room next to his   listening
and flinching praying under pillows
for my father's last grunt
for the silence of my brother's flesh

for the day I could carry all of his pain
like he had carried my sins
when he took the blame for wrecking the car
let my father beat him

that was the brother who knew love
has no opinions   who knew how lonely
the truth is   who knew brothers
have no questions about each other

I always wanted a brother
like the brother I wanted to be
but I was too busy being younger
I was too busy being the brother
neither one of us wanted to be

I always wanted to be the brother I had
so that when he came to me
on his 24th birthday   near suicide
I would say what he would say
I would do what he would do
then perhaps both of us
would still be alive

   For Bert

Isabelle

from then on
she got the motel room
while he waited in the car
she took his rage all night
bending his brown body
in the circle of her arms
that was texas

the first one
was forty-nine with long dark hairs
around her aereolas
it did not take her long
to find his twenty years
as if she had lost them in him
those were the first eighty dollars

he waited in her closet for her
because he could not stand
the way she shut him out
how she had fallen
through his flesh
came out the other side
and never looked back
that was his first jail

she had a small penis she rubbed
against his   she was tall
and liked long slow strokes always
talked and talked after
about her short Greek husband
those were the second eighty dollars

the way it started to never end
was when she brought the cat
then the champagne bottles
then the lingerie beneath the coat
then the door just opened after every breakup
that was when the end begin

he liked their eyes
she was fifty-five
she was ugly
she was a machine
she peed on him   gushed
and gushed and gushed
she still had her fundus
she said he made her lose herself
in some field of waves
she almost bit his nipple off
she smelled of her husband
she talked and talked and broke
his concentration
she was hirsute
she was quiet   stared blankly away
she always cried   spoke of her father
she wanted more
than the allotted three hours
that was rent and food and loneliness

there's a spot inside   behind
above the bone   it's not too deep
inside   you will find nothing there
except small ribs of flesh
touch it   rub it   press it
but that was texas

Sister-Mother's Adoption

I think of you tonight   Miriam
how hard it must have been
to give up all those dreams
before he had his first taste
his first memory   before he had his
first dream of you

motherless sister
who culled our father
from our sister's rooms
so they would not know
how darkness follows you

who mended our cuts and fears
held our secrets   took our blame
when we had no one but our childhoods
and yours   oldest-sister-mother

how hard it must have been to bear
such sundering   to have the choice
sink like glass shards in your belly
I've heard of how you drowned
in years   how you wandered among losses'
field of self-destructions

what scissored wind cuts us   Miriam
spreads us like dandelion seeds
to grow far apart   tonight
I know how loneliness threads us all
how we all walk in asphalt darkness

how we all dream of nighthorses
hear their shadow hooves taking us
to that place of our imagined
to watch what gives us sorrow
grow beyond our reach in weedless gardens
where stolen children play

There is a Woman

after Joy Harjo

there is a corn pollen woman
I smell in summer rains
who is sometimes red butte
sometimes skyrock
sometimes sand or prickly pear
in deserts   she is sound of air
splashing against red stone cliffs
I have woken to her singing kitchen
I have been her grain of sand
it was then I called her grandmother

there is a woman who is real
or perhaps just filaments of dreams
who is healed and unhealed wounds
who is self-reliance of an eagle's eyes
its wings   its claws
whose hands are sutures   whose voice is balm
who I thought I saw quietly mourning
at an orphan's funeral
in my memory she hears me with her heart
it is there I have called her mother

there is a woman who is secrets she keeps
who has slept with gods she called father
and brother
who is blood rain inside pomegranate skin
who has cried for silent years
checked tensions of noosed ropes
who I have called more than my sister

there is a woman who has loved
appaloosas palominos lippizaners and mustangs
who has been with horses who were broken boulders
who knows horses lie when frightened
I have danced with her   sat silent with her
walked away from her
because I thought I would remain
unbroken

there is a woman with nighthorses
who knows those horses by their imperfect
shadows who remind her of her
and in my dreams I call her
Spirit

Summer Shorts

in the shade
by the mimosa's pistachio tree trunk
grandfather sat on a poured concrete bench
its baked white paint flaking
he wore more grey and the bags
holding his age hung darkly from eyes
shuttered by glaucoma
he scanned the hot desert breeze
for sounds of his arriving past

I pulled up   brushing the curb
the mountain of frail bones rose
stepping with a blind man's tiny steps
he walked onto the scorched sidewalk
Grandfather!   we shook hands
exchanged a cautious hug
somehow   he saw me wearing
what Indians never wear summer shorts

what happened
did you forget your pants   he said
looking down at my bare legs
I began laughing   laughing
as loudly as a child laughs
when tickled by his dad's big hands

The Bodies of Shadows

a cree man once told me shadows have thicknesses
sure he said   you can stack them like dead skins
pointing that way just outside the reservation boundary
there's a whole pile of them he said   all manner of thicknesses
walking in and out of that liquor store

*   *   *   *   *   *

I know all things leave their shadows
buried in the ground   petrified in stone
after my grandfather buries the blue corn kernels in the earth
I know the shadows of the worms   insects   the winged
all the legged animals down in the sacred ground
they sing the kernels to their birth as the earth heart drums
life into them   the silent shadows sing them up out of the center
of the darkness and when they show their elongated blue-green heads
my grandfather is there with every dawning sun singing them
like he was there for us   singing us up   he sings and drums
the kernels up until they are ripe and in ceremony
we will cut them down   eat them so that the married songs of light
and darkness are reborn inside us every winter day

*   *   *   *   *   *

that redtail hawk up there dances his sacred circles gracefully
if you look at his eyes you will see his sharpness
is focused on his shadow   hawking is a lonely business
no matter how close his feathers get to the Creator's
windy voice   his earth-bound body will fill with the gravity
of loneliness   that's when you will see him dive to feed
his shadow a snared sparrow or a field mouse
that's how they keep each other company

*   *   *   *   *   *

I'm sure you too have heard of the woman crushed to death
by the shadow of her childhood   how every evening it would come
reified under the cover of darkness   how every evening
she would ask the moonlight to protect her as her mother
was never able to   how one moonless night she became so frightened
she jumped through a window trying to escape
but the shadow landed on her and crushed her   I am sure you heard
it said it was the her father's shadow but I say it was
the weight of her silence that crushed her

*   *   *   *   *   *

every dawn there is that moment when you can hear
the universal truth as silence
it happens just before the sun crests
it is the moment when all our shadows lift
off of us and you can sing their weight up
even as far as the dissolving stars
even after my grandfather has passed through
I will still hear him every dawn
out there with me   shadowless   singing
singing our shadows up   saying to them
thank you   thank you for keeping us humble
thank you   thank you for teaching us silence

The Body — Postmortem

the sutures   a crown around the skull   across the torso
black stitches outlining trapdoors to a darkened world
and the eyes are coins from an unspent life
closed for the living   opened for the dead

the boy   orphanages and foster homes   beatings and curses
of other's despairs   laughter at times but mostly silence
his unchosen word   and a young gravid wife and child whom he beat
love out of   who witnessed the cycles of nightmares end and begin

his bruise   no longer blue or purple but black
long and suffocating all about the neck
the mouth no longer crying or laughing
though pleasant   as if warmed by an unseen kiss

Desultory Moments of Ordinary Lucence

across muddy rivers of Time they arrive
in the glazed cities of reflecting panes
of glass mirroring our desert's horizon

sometimes through the scent of lilac trees
perhaps in the deadends of deserted streets that evoke
the silent speech of our moonlit conversations
the undiminished memory lit by eternal sunlight

where in rain puddles filled with tadpoles
we dance and splash you and I
with bare uncalloused feet
as if we are children woven from folklore

our thoughts yet without the madness
of those unattainable virtues
that hung from our parents eyes

Survival

for a mother I was given madness
for a father I was given absence

they raised me unclothed
in the mirrored houses of loneliness

I learned to play with my voices
which I named God and Contradiction

we lived in reservations   my brothers and sisters
who threw knives at their sad reflections

to laugh   we learned to cry
then we laughed at everything

the world was nearly 500 years old then
and had the illusion of being white and clean

God and Contradiction were the first to teach me
a game of forgiveness they called survival

Sins of Our Fathers

Why do you slay me thus unjustly;
your God will demand of you to know.
                    —Guatemozin, Moctezuma's successor

he did as he pleased   I was eight or nine
young enough to pretend I could swim
in the shallow end of his pool
in the evening   I slept on the floor
while my sisters slept on the bed
with him   that summer   I learned
what my brother had already learned
how to swim in that drowning pool

up to some less innocent year   I loved
my father for what he meant
to a child with a three week-a-year father
what he meant was my power to imagine
what he never was and would never be to me
but it was enough for me to recognize
I had been orphaned   and would someday
grow to understand what a man did not need

to be a father   yet still be called a man
it is the easiest thing to forgive
the sins of a father but harder to forget
what I feel for those he hurt
who through a new generation have passed the pains
of their guiltlessness so that they have become
their own cycle of nightmares
but I cannot absolve myself because god did not

give me a sister's young body   because god did not
make me an older brother   defiance to made an example of
I cannot absolve myself because god did not
give me the incompassionate hand
to mete out injustice and pain

I cannot absolve myself for what I have done
is nothing   except be a good listener   be someone
who must grip himself against his own incompassion

which their lives are to quick remind me of
I tell them what little I know   that I have survived
because the love I offered my father wouldn't light a candle
because god made me a witness and a son
that my guilt should run deeper than my father's
and I am nothing   not a father or a man
or a human being if I believe I can exculpate myself
from the history god and my fathers have wrought

Poem of Pain

Our nation is melting away like the snow on the
sides of the hills where the sun is warm, while your
people are like blades of grass in the spring when
summer is coming.
                                    —Red Cloud, Chief of the Oglala

I saw Chief Red Cloud standing twenty feet
from my front porch
standing on my freshly mown front lawn

he would not come inside my door
despite my motioning
I could not tempt him with my songs of horses

I saw him spread his eagle wings and fly up
(my eyes were his sharp eyes)
saw my blood in the ground   in this sacred ground

his wings gently put me down
twenty feet from him
I saw he was a boy

long blue-black hair   bronze all over him
rib bones through skin   skinny legs and arms
an orphan boy   so much abused

he was the pain   my withdrawn childhood
I felt a red wind   pass through my heart
I saw he was Red Cloud again

I smelled his love   the scent of chamomile
flowing in the breeze
between the space that separated us

I saw him smile at me   the smile of centuries
I tasted the curve of his lips
the redness of his blood

his eyes were two small Earths spinning
round and round   in his eyes
I saw life   insects   trees   a billion faces

dying   dying   leaving no traces
it was the snake that eats itself
it was the pain   the world abused

horseshadows ran out of me   his eyes were back again
I tried to speak to him
he was the two faces of my brothers

I saw their suicides   I knelt to die
it was the pain   the one that swallowed me
for twenty years   now twenty feet

I knelt to cry— I heard him sing
the chant of man
the chant of everything

there was a rainbow   stretched from me to him
across the lawn   the scent of fresh clipped grass
he was the grass   the giant maple tree

he was the sand   the desert sand
the thorny scrub
waiting patiently for me

he was the race   forty million
now almost gone
waiting patiently for me

I felt a sun set in my eye   a moon tear from my face
it was the pain of White Man Runs Him
of Tenskwátawa   the traitors regrets uplifting me

it was the pain   unhealed by time
I saw him go   heard horses running
I was my pain   it was Chief Red Cloud

I've known that pain and it was leaving me

Home—The Four-Cornered Round House

the legless sofa squats on the concrete slab
the propane apartment-stove is butted against the 2x4's
of the exposed house frame where a window looks out to a sea
of mesquité stunted by 500 years of dew for rain

the whole immense house is one
bedroom-kitchen-livingroom   the shower and the septic
in the far back corner   its the only door you can't miss it
the compressor shivers a white behemoth icebox hunched there
modernity eternally complaining   on and off off and on

the place does not have the smell of pine cleaners
the somber hum of electronically ignited gas furnaces
just the scent of sleeping babies wrapped in thin blankets
the dew collected on the timeless circles of a web
the air of wet clay   the sound of air eddies gently fading

along a dirt road   and a tarantula who every morning
when the mountains arrive in the air of lichen   moss
and streams beneath the earth   heads back to the hole
at the center of the universe and all that's left
is the sound of the sun rising in every bird

*   *   *   *   *   *   *

my home is the house made of the rosy light
that dissolves into the dust of desert watercourses
though you will not see it   the river still meanders back
to itself there   where umbilical stretches of red canyons
recede to the watery navel where we emerged without

skin or bone   before our bodies were conjured out of rain
and loam   the named was there before us   our gift
is the power to discover the sounds they make in all
of our mouths   to that end the first sacred breath of fire
was blown into our eyes that we might still see the invisible

we live here   where the past is always in front of us
and the future is changed only by the coming names   I myself
was born at that exact moment when all the celestial bodies
were moving in the circular dance of braided creations
and human destructions

not one heartbeat   not one ant was added or taken away
when I took my first crying breath   like you did

*   *   *   *   *   *   *

in that house of high ceilings
where the gargoyles of our silences
still stare wryly into our soundless hearts
where the night brought the insufferable
flesh of our father's

fantasies   how we ran through our childhood
dreams   those landscapes without impunity
inflicting upon ourselves with our fisted shames
the blue shadows that would follow us
imprinting upon ourselves   memories

without us   in his house of inverted happiness
where our leaden-hued fears spawned
into ovarian cancers and breakdowns
abuse   then divorces   into the madness
and suicides that slowly unearthed us

how we ran
from our childhoods   from our bedrooms
chasing the incorruptible flesh
taken by a father we never knew
we would never outrun or escape

*   *   *   *   *   *   *

Neches Avenue
it's a place where the asphalt deadends
one block parallel to a brown sewaged river

at night   it's the lawless faces of cops
circling   circling like great white sharks
prowling below the surface of the night
or comanches dressed in deerskins stealing quietly
to the river   creeping through neighborhood windows
for women and horses   or sacks of sacred corn to steal

in the mist of the always rising song cresting
over the dawning horizon   it's the blind old man who sits
on our front lawn   on the seams of the four-cornered world
where the sun always sings and the earth heart drums

in the darkness   it's my grandparents biding by the living-room
window listening to each other's breaths   for hours
looking down Neches Avenue   acclimating   to some new
neighborhood they only dreamed but can already see

as a boy   it's splashing in rain puddles full of tadpoles
a moon that seemed to be at each deadend I ran to
as the entire neighborhood sat out on their porches drinking
pepsi's and beers   laughing   watching the borealis clouds
from the missile range as the atomic age flew overhead
and went on by

in a dream   it's a mythical dust storm   eluviating
the last wisterias   the last lilacs precisely planted
by some grandmother's rheumatic hands as Mrs. Edgar
drives out of the swirling dust   her station wagon
windows steamed   its back heavy with the still warm
tortillas she delivered house to house

in my memory
it's all the pink and blue houses and the children
who panned out to prisons and suicides   Neches Avenue
a place which is invisible now   that I will always see
where I will always be a child beyond its name and mine

Poem Without Title

most of my life   intimacy
meant shedding my clothes
opening my fisted heart
to every smile   to every pair of eyes
that wanted part of my innocence

I thought intimacy meant giving
myself to what wounded me
never knowing what wounded me
was what I never shared with myself

in dream after murderous dream
I have tried to avenge the incest
the beatings   the abandonment
left by my father

never forgetting myself in the slightest
chance of forgiveness   I have tried to destroy
that one indestructible moment
when as a child   I saw my father's
love for me

once   I was rooted in a land
of grandfathers and grandmothers
before the time of contradictions
before first grade   before I begin
to be a hieroglyph   undeciphered
lost   even to myself

for so long I have walked with ghosts
searching their pained voices for forgiveness
only to find forgiveness is the silent
voice of my heart

Curbstone Press, Inc.
is a non-profit publishing house dedicated to literature that reflects
a commitment to social change, with an emphasis on contemporary
writing from Latin America and Latino communities in the United
States. Curbstone presents writers who give voice to the unheard in
a language that goes beyond denunciation to celebrate, honor and
teach. Curbstone builds bridges between its writers and the public –
from inner-city to rural areas, colleges to community centers, children
to adults. Curbstone seeks out the highest aesthetic expression of the
dedication to human rights and intercultural understanding: poetry,
testimonials, novels, stories, photography.

This mission requires more than just producing books. It requires
ensuring that as many people as possible know about these books and
read them. To achieve this, a large portion of Curbstone's schedule is
dedicated to arranging tours and programs for its authors, working
with public school and university teachers to enrich curricula,
reaching out to underserved audiences by donating books and
conducting readings and community programs, and promoting
discussion in the media. It is only through these combined efforts that
literature can truly make a difference.

Curbstone Press, like all non-profit presses, depends on the support of
individuals, foundations, and government agencies to bring you, the
reader, works of literary merit and social significance which might not
find a place in profit-driven publishing channels. Our sincere thanks
to the many individuals who support this endeavor and to the
following foundations and government agencies: ADCO Foundation,
J. Walton Bissell Foundation, Inc., Witter Bynner Foundation for
Poetry, Inc., Connecticut Commission on the Arts, Connecticut Arts
Endowment Fund, Lannan Foundation, LEF Foundation, Lila
Wallace-Reader's Digest Fund, The Andrew W. Mellon Foundation,
National Endowment for the Arts-Literature, National Endowment
for the Arts International Projects Initiative and The Plumsock Fund.

Please support Curbstone's efforts to present the diverse voices and
views that make our culture richer. Tax-deductible donations can be
made to Curbstone Press, 321 Jackson Street, Willimantic, CT 06226.